A Daymare of Violence

Brenda Moore

Grosvenor House
Publishing Limited

All rights reserved
Copyright © Brenda Moore, 2023

The right of Brenda Moore to be identified as the author of this
work has been asserted in accordance with Section 78
of the Copyright, Designs and Patents Act 1988

The book cover is copyright to Brenda Moore

This book is published by
Grosvenor House Publishing Ltd
Link House
140 The Broadway, Tolworth, Surrey, KT6 7HT.
www.grosvenorhousepublishing.co.uk

This book is sold subject to the conditions that it shall not, by way of
trade or otherwise, be lent, resold, hired out or otherwise circulated
without the author's or publisher's prior consent in any form of
binding or cover other than that in which it is published and
without a similar condition including this condition being
imposed on the subsequent purchaser.

A CIP record for this book
is available from the British Library

ISBN 978-1-80381-451-3

Dedication

My book is dedicated to all the men and women of Ballyfermot, Dublin, who experienced a tough time at our respective Catholic primary schools where corporal punishment was the norm throughout the 1960s. We are the survivors of continuous and systematic abuse by the religious orders and lay teachers who taught us back then and at primary school level.

***

'We cannot find peace until we find all the pieces'

All proceeds from the sale of this book will go towards two charities that support socially disadvantaged and underprivileged children.

La Canasta de Amistad	YES Uganda
(The Friendship Basket)	Fort Portal
Lima	Uganda
Peru	

Acknowledgement

I would like to extend my gratitude to Ken Larkin, Secretary of the Ballyfermot Heritage Group who encouraged me, in the first instance, to write down my story in order to heal from my past. Thank you Ken for your kindness.

I would also like to acknowledge Barry Cullen from Rialto, Dublin. Barry your support throughout was invaluable. You helped me to tell my story in the way that I wanted it to be told. I am forever grateful to you. Thank you so much.

Introduction

I grew up in Ballyfermot, Dublin, Ireland, in the sixties, and in 'A Daymare of Violence', I outline my experience of physical abuse and torment at my primary school between 1960-67. I was regularly physically beaten by my class teacher, and each day I carried the dread and fear that it would be one of those days. Most of the violence centred around my inability as a child to grasp and complete basic arithmetic exercises. Knowing that I could not understand the arithmetic tasks meant that I simply waited for the next bout of violence arising from these failures. Here I describe the psychological and emotional impact of this violence; its effect on me at the time, and also the prolonged and continuous impact in later life.

In my fifties I addressed my fear of maths through study and examination. However, the scar of violence remained with me for decades and still has a disturbing effect on my emotions and well-being. I have worked through these issues but only insofar as I could on an individual basis. Ultimately, it will take others – particularly the institutions that were so central to my childhood school experience – to address the pain, hurt, and violence caused and its aftermath, and to address the culture of silence that surrounded the use of violence with young children… and the legacy it has left.

My Story

In 1960, at the age of six, I was happily walking along the street holding my mother's hand when we turned into a huge yard where a group of mothers and their children were standing. Many of the children were crying, screaming, and kicking, as I looked on bewildered. I had no idea what was happening, what was wrong, or why these children were so upset. As the scene unfolded, I became even more frightened and I firmly gripped my mother's hand.

Some women came forward and took the children, then walked them across the yard. It seemed that, like me, the children did not know who these women were, nor where they intended to take us. Many of the children pulled away from the women, kicking out and screaming. Their distress unsettled me, especially as it dawned on me that I too would be taken.

Eventually, a woman came forward to take me. Like the other children, I did not want to go, but I had no choice. My mother bent down towards me and said in a quiet voice, "You will be alright. I will come back for you at lunch time." And with that she offered this stranger my hand, which was still tightly gripping hers.

I expect my mother must have tried to prepare me for school, but I do not remember her doing so. I knew nothing about what to expect. Up until then I had been happy, cocooned in my own little world at home at our house.

My family arrived in Ballyfermot from Dublin's city centre in 1949. At the time my parents had three young children; they eventually went on to have nine. I was the sixth and was born at home on Landen Road in 1954. As an infant and a young child, my mother was the centre of my world, and that world was a happy one. I simply existed as part of this large, noisy family where nothing was demanded of me and I demanded nothing of myself. I watched daily events unfold around me with great curiosity and joyfulness. As the child in the middle, I did not belong to the first half of my siblings, nor did I belong to the second half; one group was a lot older, and the other a lot younger. And I came in between two boys, with whom I had little in common. I was not interested in playing with boys anyway.

I felt alone much of the time, but that did not matter much since my main interest and focus was on my mother and just being around her. I was happy in the knowledge that I was safe and secure at home and under her care. She was endlessly busy carrying out her daily chores: cleaning, cooking, washing clothes, and caring for her large family. My mother would sing to her heart's content throughout the house as she went about her tasks. She always appeared upbeat, and her singing created a nice ambience in the house. My mother's joyfulness reflected on me when I was a young child and gave me a feeling of warmth and contentment. At that period in time, my home environment was such that I felt wrapped up in a little bubble of warmth.

My four older sisters left school at 14 years of age, which was common in working class communities prior to the introduction of free secondary education in 1967. They all went to work in manufacturing, and I have memories of them bringing home a wage to give to my mother every week, thereby easing the financial burden. I also remember them coming in from work for the evening meal.

There was always a lot of happy chatter and giggling between them and my mother, and they appeared to me to be very happy, fun loving, and gregarious young teenagers. They created a nice atmosphere at home, and although I was too young to be included in their circle, I was content to sit on the side-lines and watch them happily and excitedly interact. They seemed to all get along very well.

I remember in the middle of winter my sisters and my mother would sit in a semi-circle around a blazing hot open coal fire in the sitting room, knitting and chatting the evening away. One of the advantages of having older sisters was that they were skilled at hand knitting, so I was never without a lovely jumper or cardigan to wear. After a few years I was able to join them, and with their tuition I could eventually knit my own Aran jumpers. I was also able to contribute to making knitted baby garments for my nephews and nieces who followed later.

As a young child, I watched my father come and go from work. He was very happy when he had employment, but when he had no work, he was like a bear with a sore head. He was a labourer, and he took any and every job that came his way. Contract work was common back then, though, which meant he was regularly laid off. When that happened, he would walk the streets day after day to look for more work. He was made redundant numerous times – a common occurrence back then – but each time he bounced back, never a quitter, and with just one thought in mind which was to find work and bring home money to feed his family.

There was a period when my father would travel to work by bicycle. I would ask my mother the time and when it was near 6pm, the time my father was due home from work, I would sit on the steps at the front of the house and keep watch for his return. I was a daddy's girl for a long time. I could not contain myself, and as the time drew nearer I would walk down the road just a block away in anticipation of his approach. When I would spot him in the distance, I would run down the road to greet him. He would lift me up and place me on the handlebars of his bicycle and give me a little jaunt back up the road to our house. It did not matter that the handlebars were cold and hard to sit on. This was a real treat; I loved it, and he never disappointed.

Every so often my father would take us to town to visit his parents, who lived in Ringsend. My grandfather sold the *Evening Herald* on the street, and he would keep new and shiny pennies to give to us when we visited. My grandparents had a budgie called Joey, which was a great novelty to us. We spent a lot of time trying to get Joey to talk, but he was more inclined to squawk. We persisted, though, convinced that he would eventually talk back to us.

My father also sometimes took me to visit my grandmother, and then all three of us would go to a pub where they both drank Guinness while I had orange juice and crisps. The pub always stank of stale tobacco. Although my grandmother never spoke to me, she would always look at me lovingly, scrutinise my face, and tell my father that I was the image of her eldest daughter. I enjoyed those outings very much where just the fact of being there and feeling included was enough for me.

Every August, my father took us to the Royal Dublin Horse Show in Ballsbridge. It was a special outing for us, and I particularly enjoyed the dressage as well as the ice-cream treats that we got. He also regularly took us to the Oriel (Majestic) cinema in Chapelizod, to the side of the old Garda Station. Our walk from Landen Road took us down Lynch's Lane – a narrow, steep country laneway that started between the two schools. It is no longer there.

We saw old comedy films, including *Old Mother Riley* – a drag act in which the central character wore an ankle-length dress, a bonnet, and black laced-up ankle boots. She got into all sorts of mischief, similar to the Mr Bean character of today. The cinema also played *The Three Stooges* and *Laurel and Hardy*.

It would be quite dark on the way home, especially as Lynch's Lane was badly lit. But with my hand in my father's, I would chat away happily, and he would say "Oh, is that right?" and similar such responses. Looking back, I wonder if he ever listened to a word I said. We never actually held a conversation, but I thought he was listening, and that was all that mattered.

My father had a tattoo on his upper right arm of a lady wearing a bikini. Her feet were pointed downwards, and she wore ballet shoes. He would shake the skin on his arm and make her dance to entertain us. He was amused at how this intrigued us, and when he stopped, we would pester him to make her dance again. We were mesmerised; it was like watching a show.

My father had the voice of a tenor and, like my mother, he was a keen singer, spending most Saturday afternoons locked away in the parlour listening to Pavarotti, Carreras, and Domingo, on his record player, sometimes singing along while looking out of the window onto the street. I remember him singing *Because* (*God made thee mine*) by Mario Lanza, and now that he is deceased, it is the one song that reminds me of him whenever I hear it.

On Saturday nights my parents would dress up in their finest clothes and spend the evening singing and dancing at Tolka Lodge in Glasnevin with extended family and friends, as most were from the northside, mainly Finglas and Santry. My father was a shy person while my mother was an extravert; I guess in that way they complemented each other. My mother would sing songs made famous by the late singer, David Alexander. *(Love is All)* or the late John McCormack (*Little Town in the Old County Down)*. If she was feeling more gregarious, she would sing *Y Viva España* while she flicked her circular skirt from side to side like a Spanish señora performing a flamenco dance. They were a fun-loving group of people who made their own entertainment.

As Friday was my father's pay day, we always had a small party on Friday evenings, with ice cream in a mug and lemonade poured on top to create a thick fizzy cream which had to be eaten with a spoon as it was like a meal in a cup! It was a bonus to have ice cream wafers, and it was the best treat ever. My father would also give us pocket money which we called our pay. We did nothing to deserve payment, but when it was pay day for him it was pay day for us children too. If I thought it was getting late and maybe he had forgotten, I would approach him and say, "Da, can I have my pay please?" It was usually about six old pence. From our pay, we would buy sweets such as aniseed balls, also known as Nancy balls, hard-boiled sweets such as bulls' eyes, cloves, and acid drops, and also strings of liquorice and Peggy's legs.

In general, my recollections of early childhood are very positive, and some of this positivity remained with me through my life. School changed everything, however. It totally disrupted my overall sense of wholeness and confidence, and took me decades to recover. For me, that day when I was taken across the yard in the Dominican Convent

Primary School, Ballyfermot, was the start of a nightmare. But because all the events took place during the daytime, I called it my *daymare.*

The school was run by the Dominican Order of nuns, teaching sisters, and it also had some female lay teachers – mostly new graduates from teaching colleges. To the best of my knowledge, my primary school teacher – a lay teacher by the name of Miss Keane[1] – taught me right through the seven years I was there. She was from Limerick. Most teachers, nuns included, were young people, and probably in their twenties.

My first experience of physical abuse happened shortly after I started school. We were being taken down to the toilets in single file, and I could see Miss Keane at the top of the line; I was halfway down. I turned around to speak to the child behind me, and as I did, I got an unmerciful blow to the back of my right leg. I felt a sharp pain and stinging sensation, and before I could turn fully around again to see what had happened, the teacher screamed into my ear, "I said no talking!"

---

[1] Miss Keane is a pseudonym.

She was right; she had said that, but I froze in fear. I was dazed and my leg buzzed with pain. I could not understand how she could have been so far away at the top of the line one minute and right beside me and up close physically the next. I was stunned to find her towering over me and shocked by her loud and aggressive voice. I had never experienced such aggression and shouting before that event.

I knew and understood the reason for my punishment. I had heard her shout out from the top of the queue "No talking" and I had ignored her. I had spoken when I should not have, and because of that I felt it was my own fault and that I deserved this punishment, that I deserved to be humiliated, exposed, and vulnerable in front of the other girls.

This was my introduction into the school, but it was to get worse. It was my first wallop, but only the start of many more severe and hard slaps and a lot of physical and emotional abuse where I was set upon by my teacher. Her weapons of choice were her large adult hands, the blackboard pointer, and the 12-inch ruler. This was when my daymares began.

My teacher clamped down on me, suppressing my spirit, causing me endless days of anxiety, fear, and beatings. I was no longer cocooned in the warmth of my childhood. Instead, my eyes were opened to a world where I experienced fear and anxiety on a daily basis, and I lived them out day after day.

My fears always began on my way to school. I would feel apprehensive, especially as I did not know what to expect from one day to the next, or even from one moment to the next when I got there. And as the day progressed, my fears mounted. It never crossed my mind to make friends with other children. It was not encouraged, in any case. We did not seem to be there for each other, but just to learn – nothing more. Other children existed around me like shadows. I was preoccupied with beatings, anticipating them, and wondering how I could avoid them. My focus was on my teacher alone and the fear I held from not knowing what she might do next, or what she might beat me with next.

Miss Keane beat me primarily for not being able to work out my sums. Each day she gave us ten arithmetic sums for homework, and the next day ten pupils were randomly called to work out one of the sums on the blackboard. On my turns, she beat me continuously because I could not do my sums.

I had already clammed up after my first experience of physical abuse, as I quickly learned that it was easier to remain silent, hoping to become less visible and go unnoticed in a 40-pupil classroom, and to avoid beatings. Because of fear and anxiety, I became introverted, remaining quiet throughout primary school. Unintentionally, I isolated myself from the other girls, and I became sad and confused. But mostly, I grew in fear. I was no longer the contented child I remembered being before school, but was becoming something else mainly because I just could not comprehend or understand sums. And I had no sense that the teacher made any allowance for this.

I remember crying in bed one night, feeling frustrated because I could not get around this problem. My younger brother, just a child himself, wandered into my bedroom and asked me, "Why are you crying?" I replied, "I can't do my sums," but he just toddled off out again and my upset went unnoticed.

Halves and quarters made sense to me, but otherwise fractions had me completely baffled.

I just saw a whole load of numbers separated by a line. They all drew from the same structure, and since I was unable to complete one scenario, I was unable to complete any. Typically, scenarios were about farmers who divided their land amongst their sons, and there would be questions about the fraction of the land that the farmer kept for himself. Aside from not understanding fractions, I had little understanding of farmers or why they would divide their land with their sons. I just could not relate to the scenarios. My mind was completely in the dark, a total blank, and my feelings of fear and terror did little to allow me to see more clearly.

I have no recollection of Miss Keane attempting to explain how to work out these sums, and if she did so, it all went over my head. I remember one girl who never got a sum wrong when she was called to the blackboard. She would pick up the chalk and work out the sum from start to finish without hesitation and then produce the correct answer. I never ever got a sum right and she never ever got a sum wrong!

She was the only girl who could take my focus off my teacher. She fascinated me, and I wanted to know how she could see through all those numbers the way that I could not. I could not understand why there was a blank in my head, complete and utter darkness, when I tried so hard to relax and push through that darkness and work out the sums.

As a young child, I would lie in bed frustrated and crying, asking myself why it was that I could not do this homework. But no answers ever came. I remained in a continuous state of anxiety, in fear and frustration, day after day and night after night. It was a quiet and miserable existence locked in my own world with my own thoughts, and I have no sense that anybody noticed how unhappy I was. It was not a family habit to ask for support with homework, and no help was ever offered. Home was home and school was school, and they did not meet.

My mother, in any case, was permanently busy doing all the physical work involved in running the household, and because it was a large family it was hard to be seen and heard. It seemed that only my older siblings had a say in conversations. I was never encouraged to speak, and as far as I can recall I did not have conversations with my mother or any other family members when I was a child. My mother never asked how my day at school went, and I never offered any information. If I appeared to be okay physically, then all was right. The emotional side simply went unnoticed, so my unhappiness was never discussed nor addressed. I just came and went to school, and it was something I did which was separate from my home life.

I accepted that my teacher and all the teaching staff and nuns were in charge of me while I was in their care, and although I was unhappy about it, I accepted the abuse without bringing home tales. It just wasn't the done thing. I felt trapped; there was nothing I could do to end the madness in my life.

On my way to school, I was always apprehensive and full of fear, not knowing what the day would bring. Would my teacher be in today? Would she call me to the blackboard to work out a sum? If she did, that would mean a definite beating. Would she be absent, and the class divided up? Would I be sent to Miss Rabbit's classroom, where Miss Rabbit[2] would put the fear of God into me and possibly thump me on my back? Miss Rabbit

---

[2] Miss Rabbit is a pseudonym.

punished the girls in her classroom when they got the wrong answer by making a fist and thumping them on their upper back. The girls would be standing up beside their desks at this point.

I don't know which was more terrifying for me, whether my teacher was in school or absent. Facing each school day just filled me with fear and dread. As I walked to school, I could feel a heavy weight pressed against my chest. Coming home was the same, knowing that I had to do ten more sums for homework, and I always knew that the next day I would be facing the same anxiety. I would put it behind me for a few hours until later in the evening when I attempted to do my homework once again, and the frustration would build up in me once more. This was an impossible task for me.

I would think about my dilemma last thing at night before sleep, and first thing each morning and all morning until maths class was over. My daymares were plentiful and kept my mind well occupied. It was a vicious cycle and I felt trapped, frustrated and very unhappy.

My emotional turmoil, frustration, and upset would increase as the day progressed, until finally the maths session began and I would sit bolt upright and in complete terror. The moment I had dreaded had arrived. This was the climax of my day, and everything before this period was a build-up to this moment. Miss Keane would scan the room and randomly pick out a girl to execute a sum on the blackboard.

I would sit there, hot and tense, my heart thumping in my chest, feeling sick in my stomach. I must have said in my head a million times, whilst twisting my fingers in my lap, *Oh, please God, don't let her ask me, don't let her ask me, oh please God!* I'd work myself into a frenzy. Then, when she called out some other girl's name, I would slump back in relief and take a few moments to breathe normally again… until the next sum was due to be done, and the fear would surge up inside of me once again. I continued pleading with God until the maths session was over, and only then was I able to relax for the rest of the day and involve myself in the subjects that followed, particularly Irish, English and Catechism, none of which I found complicated.

Inevitably Miss Keane would call out my name, and I would freeze at the sound, with my name hanging in the air. You could hear a pin drop in the classroom. The moment I dreaded had come.

It had been only a matter of time. The blood drained from my body and my heart thumped in my chest, as I knew only too well what was to follow. Slowly I would rise from my desk with my exercise book in my hand, where my pathetic attempts at doing my sums homework was written down, then I would walk to the blackboard like I was walking to a guillotine. My head was totally blank. Fear gripped my entire body. I really don't know how I didn't faint at times with the feelings of sheer terror that I experienced in those awful moments after she called my name.

On reaching the blackboard, I would pick up the chalk with my left hand, being a *ciotóg*[3], and I would attempt to write out the sum on the board. I would write on the blackboard the fractions suggested in the sum, adding the plus sign between them, or the minus sign, whichever I thought was the correct one. After that, I was totally clueless as to how to work through the sum.

It was the same scenario every time. I would put down the chalk at this point, which was my signal to

---

[3] Irish word for left-handed.

her that I could go no further, and it was then that she would pounce.

Normally she would be standing by the window, leaning against the radiator, and watching me from halfway down the room. When I put down the chalk, she would charge up the room towards me like a raging bull. All I could do was stand there and await her approach and her attack. When she reached me, she would pull up my skirt to my embarrassment, as all the girls could see my knickers, and then she would slap me severely and repeatedly on my thighs with her big adult hand. She slapped me so severely that my knees would buckle from the force of the blows, and I would have to grip tightly onto the edge of the blackboard in order to remain upright.

I don't ever remember crying during this abuse; mostly I felt numb and in shock, but I still remember that it was excruciatingly painful to be beaten on the back of my thighs. I was trapped there, almost pinned to the wall and blackboard, just gripping on tightly lest I fall down. And I had to bide my time until she was satiated.

After a time, and when the beatings became a regular occurrence, I learned somehow to separate my mind from my body and this allowed me to cope a little better with the pain. I would close my eyes whilst hanging onto the blackboard edge, and as she beat me I would allow my mind to float away from my body somewhere out there to distance myself from the pain. I taught myself a form of escapism, and it helped to some degree. It seemed to take the edge off the pain.

Miss Keane continued to slap my bare thighs until her anger abated. Once she finished, I would sit back down at my desk feeling humiliated, sad, and miserable. I never felt I was stupid or slow, because I could cope perfectly well with the other subjects. It was more a sense of great mystery, confusion, and frustration, as to why I could not do these sums when I could clearly see that other pupils could do them without any problem.

Occasionally during maths class, Miss Keane would be seated at her desk near the blackboard when she would call me out to execute a sum. After I gave her the signal by putting down the chalk to let her know that I could go no further with the sum, she would reach over and drag me by my arm to where she was sitting. Then she would pull me across her knee, again pull up my skirt, and beat me severely on my bare thighs. I may have been a little older then – maybe eight or nine at that stage – although I cannot say exactly. I remember that despite being small for my age, my teacher was clumsy in her attempts to pull me across her lap. I was aware that this was wrong, and I felt too old to be put across her knee. I felt humiliated with the whole class looking on, and also embarrassed and angry because I felt she was treating me like a baby.

This punishment felt so wrong, and sometimes she was so awkward that I almost fell off her lap. My body would wobble as I was sprawled across her lap, and my breathing would be laboured as part of my chest and my belly were pressed down on her lap. I felt awkward and unbalanced on top of her lap.

On one occasion, an important shift took place in my psyche, and I found it within myself to say "no" inside, to defy her for the first time. She was seated behind her desk, and as she dragged me across to where she was sitting, and before she pulled me across her lap, my left side, my more dominant side, was furthest away from her. I discovered that if I reached out and placed my left hand on her desk in front of us, as long as I kept my arm straight and didn't bend my elbow, she would have difficulty in pulling me across her lap. Of course, when she realised my left arm was straight, she overpowered me by simply tugging at me and pulling me with greater force until her strength overcame mine and she had me where she wanted me, prostrated across her lap.

I always knew that what she was doing was wrong, and although I would not dare to answer her back, I had found a non-verbal way to object. It never stopped her from carrying out this physical abuse, but it gave me confidence and strength to know that I had stood up to her, even if only in a small way. In my defiance I felt strong and brave, and that felt good.

During Catechism class, we would all stand in single file by the window. Miss Keane would test us to see if we knew our catechism homework with a question-and-answer session. We were expected to regurgitate the answers, and woe betide any girl who had not done her homework or who could not learn by repetition. You either knew the answers off by heart, or you did not. You could not bluff your way out of it, and if you didn't know the answer, you took your punishment.

I was good at learning parrot-fashion, so most of the time I felt confident that I knew the answers to the questions. However, I still feared that my mind would go blank and my nerves might get the better of me at the last minute. On occasion, this actually happened. I knew the answer but my mind would go blank through fear, and I was then slapped.

Normally, the punishment was a hard slap with a 12-inch ruler on the palm of each hand, or two hard slaps on each hand if the teacher so desired. These slaps felt like a short, sharp shock, and as with every other child who was hit with the ruler, the slaps left the palms of our hands red and with a stinging, painful sensation. This type of punishment was commonplace; a daily occurrence.

Miss Keane also liked to use the blackboard pointer to hit me across the palms of my hands when I did not know the answers. The blackboard pointer was a wooden stick, approximately 20 inches long. The handle was thick, and it graduated into a point. We called it the roly-poly stick because it was round in shape. "Put out your hand," she would say without any emotion. I would extend my arm sideways, offering her the palm of my hand to be slapped. Whack! Down would come the stick, and bounce off my little hand. "Now the other one!" she would say just as coldly, then she would proceed to hit me on the palm of my other hand. My hands truly felt like she had broken them. The stick would sometimes come down on the bend of my thumb right on the bone, in that area of my thumb where there is no padding, and it would remain painful for hours.

I felt battered and bruised, as though my hands were broken and paralysed. My hands would feel as though they were on fire, red marks would appear across my palms, and a stabbing pain and warmth would emanate from them. I would remain in a numbed state for the whole afternoon, with both my hands resting on my lap, palms upwards, and feeling like my whole being had been crushed. I would feel lightheaded and devastated, and I really don't know how I survived the blackboard pointer.

The pain of that stick took me beyond my endurance and pain threshold. I would cry and be in pain the whole afternoon. I would look up at her, and I would say over and over in my mind, *I hate you; I really hate you!* as the tears rolled down my cheeks. She would resume the lesson and simply carry on and ignore me, as if the abuse had never happened.

Miss Keane was a very cold and unforgiving person. She taught me the kind of things that should have no place in a young child's world. She taught me again and again how to feel fear, anger, hatred, terror, frustration, and anxiety. Her treatment of me diminished my sense of identity, my dignity, and my self-worth.

At about eleven years of age, I took an interest in swinging on the concrete lamp post which stood on the pavement outside of our house. It was a very enjoyable pastime, a counter to the drudgery of school, and I never grew tired of it. I would swing for what seemed like hours at a time. One of the boys would climb up the lamp post, pushing the rope up before him as he went, then securing the rope high up on the thick concrete post. I did try once to climb the post, but I just couldn't get off the ground!

Once the rope was secure, I would spend the afternoon on the swing and not go back into the house until teatime. I loved my time swinging on the lamp post and the sense of freedom it gave me to abandon myself to the elements, swinging higher and higher up and around the post, until I was caught way up high. With no more rope left, I would be suspended up high, hugging the concrete post like a bear. I would then freefall backwards and let the elements take me back down again, around and around, until my feet touched the ground.

It was a great sensation to feel free in space and time, to have a sense of oneness with myself and the world. I had a feeling of complete peace and calm when I was swinging through the air and freefalling back down. I could feel the warmth of the summer breeze blowing through my hair, touching my skin and wrapping itself around my body. I lived in the moment of space and time, and I thought about nothing. I was completely relaxed and without a care in the world. It was a feeling of bliss!

At around the same age, my mother bought me a Christmas present of a pair of roller skates, which had four thick rubber wheels. They were the best kind, the elite of roller skates, and made for stability and speed. Skating was just as much fun as swinging on the lamp post, because I could abandon myself to the elements and feel the breeze against my face and my whole body.

There was no-one pulling me back, talking me down, or beating me up!

I was outdoors, doing what I loved best and feeling totally free and at peace with myself. There always seemed to be a nice warm breeze that touched my face and brushed off my bare arms and legs as I skated along, building up as much speed as I could muster. It was a warmth that wrapped itself around me and cocooned me like a close friend. As I free-wheeled down the tarmac hill, skating took me off to another dimension. These were mostly solitary pastimes. Although my two childhood friends had skates, they were not attracted to the speed element of skating, so mostly I had to leave them behind as I sped off, though I would come back and join them every so often. Those long, warm summers as a child, and the pastimes I took part in, were possibly the best times of my childhood.

In 1967, at the age of 13, I left primary school for the Dominican Convent secondary school, and I felt as though I had been released from hell! A weight was lifted off me, and I felt like I could breathe properly at school for the first time and relax. The madness had ended, but it took much more time after that to steady myself and calm my emotions. It probably took the best part of my first year at secondary school to begin to feel a semblance of normality.

I never saw Miss Keane again, nor did I ever think of her throughout my secondary school years. I had a lot of new subjects to distract me, and I enjoyed having many different teachers come in and out of the classroom to teach their specific subject.

A new world had opened up for me at secondary school. There was no corporal punishment administered, since it was replaced by the use of detention and the writing of lines as a deterrent for wrong-doing. For the first time I began to enjoy attending school and learning new things. I would say, in fact, that my education only really began from my first year in secondary school. All in all, it was a relief to be out of the hell of primary school and to begin my learning in a different environment. I was able to bury my bad experiences and to put Miss Keane right out of my mind – for this period of my life anyway.

I never progressed at maths, since I did not have the foundation, so I failed maths in both the

Intermediate and Leaving Certificate (equivalent to O and A Levels). I was never able to shift that mental block I experienced. I had built up the habit of being fearful and frustrated before I attempted the sums, so it took all that I had to break down that wall of darkness and try to comprehend. But I never fully broke away from that fear, so maths remained a no-go area for me until many decades later.

In contrast to my primary school teacher, who disturbed and upset me to the extreme, my English teacher Miss Joy[4] in my final year at secondary school was the finest teacher I had ever known. Unfortunately, it took me until my last year at school to connect with a teacher who made a very strong and positive impact on me. She enlightened me like no other teacher had ever done, and opened a window for me to the world of English literature, of plays, prose, and sonnets. I was enthralled, totally captivated, like never before, and she kept me engaged for all of sixth year. She made literature come alive and broke down poetry in all its paragraphs, sentences, and words, finding all the hidden meanings of what the poet was trying to

---
[4] Miss Joy is a pseudonym.

convey to the reader with subtle tones and meaning, the writings full of nuances. The style and language used in poetry and prose had to be studied to be understood, and she knew how to convey its every message to us. We studied Shakespeare's *Hamlet,* and the boys up the road in the technical school staged the play. Some of us girls went to see them and had a good laugh as the boys pranced around the stage in their black tights and pumpkin-like pants from the Shakespearean era. Thanks to her, I came to love the English language and English literature.

To this day, there are poems and parts of *Hamlet* that I can recite through my love of literature. And although my English teacher came along a little late, I have always been grateful for the one year I had with her. She was to me the epitome of what a teacher should be. She knew her subject thoroughly, how to convey it, and also how to get the best out of us. She knew how to teach, and she marked our work fairly. Miss Joy treated us all equally.

Although it was a struggle for me to get through secondary school, including failing my Inter Cert, I had become hungry for knowledge and was determined not to leave school as a failure.

I ploughed on and studied hard, and in the summer of 1972 – at 18 years of age – I passed the Leaving Certificate.

I was pleased with my results and particularly with passing Art, because I had failed it at the Intermediate exam despite studying hard. At last, I felt equal to everyone else. I was happy at this stage to leave school and embark on my life out in the wider world, determined I would always do my work to the best of my ability.

It was later in my life that I found that Miss Keane had left her imprint etched deep inside me. She seemed to be represented by a dark shadow that stayed and walked with me and affected me throughout my adult life. She was the negativity I experienced every so often, reinforcing my low self-esteem. She was the small voice that whispered to me, "No you can't do it, don't even try. You cannot do it, you will never make it!" But I was a fighter, so I kept battling off this negative force despite its constant presence, and I carried on in a positive light.

I don't say this lightly. It was not an easy thing to do, as her shadowy presence refused to go away, and the poor self-esteem had become embedded.

It took decades and willpower to develop my confidence before I overcame this negativity and turned my life around. I would say, in fact, it took the best part of my adult life to develop into the person I was meant to be.

During secondary school, and for a while after, I had considered studying nursing. Indeed, I succeeded at my nursing interview and was offered a place, provided I got my Leaving Certificate. Despite my interest, I allowed others, including family members and a nun from the school, to pour cold water on the idea, and eventually I talked myself out of it.

I had already started work in an office, as I was good with touch typing and my English was also good. I met others my own age there, and we had a good social life. However, I later regretted that I had not followed my dream, that I had over-listened to others, and that my own lack of confidence had gotten the better of me. It was one of the first of life's lessons, and it taught me to get in touch with and listen to myself. It was a hard lesson to learn, but it served me well later in life.

My typing proficiency improved, especially when I acquired an IBM golfball typewriter. My confidence in the office also grew, and I was able to move successfully through a number of secretarial and administrative roles. I carried an aversion to maths, and everything associated with it, however, right into my early fifties. The very idea of maths, even the word itself, would arouse so many bad feelings in the pit of my stomach and make my tummy churn. I could not look at anything that resembled numbers and calculations, although I was very astute when it came to managing my own finances. I felt so bad that I would grimace to emphasise how much I hated maths, and put my hands over my eyes in an attempt to block out the past horrific images that came to mind at that very word.

As a secretary, I worked hard and with a lot of intensity, mainly on long technical reports for architects, insurance companies, and engineers. My bosses had very high standards and I found they were very strict, so I knew that if they were happy with my work I must be doing something right. As a result, I could feel pleased with myself, and my confidence grew.

Yet, when asked to cast an eye over some invoices, I would immediately have a physical reaction. My heart would thump, my blood would rush around my body, my face would feel hot and flushed, and I would feel sick in the pit of my stomach. My inner voice would scream out, "Oh no, no maths. Please, no." And a mocking voice inside would holler at me, "Ha! Let's see what you can do now!"

I would have to do some self-talk, tell myself to stay calm, that it's really easy. And in truth, I knew it was. I just had to get past the initial fear that gripped me and stopped me from being able to function in the normal sense. I could not tell my boss that I did not want to go anywhere near his invoices. That just wasn't the done thing! You did not say "no" to any task given to you at work unless you wanted to be shown the door.

As the decades rolled by, I became sick of hearing myself say, "I hate maths." I had read the book, *Feel the Fear and Do it Anyway* by Susan Jeffers, and this prompted me to take up the gauntlet and study GCSE maths in my adopted home in London. I was in my early fifties at this point and I studied for two years in a college in London where, to my astonishment, I found that I really enjoyed the challenge.

The first evening I walked into the college classroom, that same old rush of fear came over me and I felt sick in my stomach. I was angry with myself, and kept thinking that I had to stop this nonsense. I knew it was ridiculous to have these physical reactions some 40 years after my primary school days!

I explained to my teacher about my past experiences of maths, and she promised not to beat me, which made me laugh and it broke the ice. I sat down in the classroom, my heart still thumping, my face flushed, and feeling uncomfortable, despite knowing nothing sinister would happen to me. But somehow I pushed through my fear.

As time went on, I relaxed, and I actually found it interesting to work out the problems. Even the times when I found the maths difficult, it did not faze me and I was able to keep a cool head. I did not get the old feelings of frustration and the need to beat myself up.

I persevered and I worked steadily at my subject, facing the challenge head on – and I succeeded. It was probably my best ever life achievement to simply pass my GCSE maths exam. How I would love to have met Ms Keane then and waved my certificate at her. I felt even more proud of myself when I later learned that the majority of the students in the class were repeating the second year to try and achieve the grade I had achieved the first time around.

In the summer of 2003, and in my fifties, I proudly accepted my first official maths certificate. I had a GCSE in maths! Release the balloons! Success at last!

Workwise, my adult life has mostly been lived in the fast lane, continuously on the go from my twenties through to my fifties, and my thinking and relaxation time usually came while I lay in bed awaiting sleep. On the odd occasion when sleep eluded me, thoughts of my formative years would quite unexpectedly flash across my mind, and I would find myself revisiting that dark place of my childhood. From my vantage point, I would look down and watch myself in that classroom, the miserable, unhappy child that I was, and I would shed a few tears in the darkness of my bedroom for the times when I was filled with such hopelessness and despair with no escape from that cruel cycle of abusive events.

It would have been good to travel back there, sit beside the young version of me in the classroom, give my child self a hug, and tell her to hang on in there, that this torment wouldn't last forever. Or better still, whisper to her to speak with her mother, tell her everything that was happening, and not to wait a day longer before speaking with her.

After such nights, I would wake the next morning, leave the nightmare behind me, and continue my life's journey in its usual hectic fashion. My bad dreams would be suppressed and negative thoughts put behind me until another time when my daymares would come back and revisit me before sleep.

That seven-year period of being beaten instilled in me a strong sense of not being good enough, and that my attempts at being good enough were thwarted, because alongside the beatings I was also *taught* that I was not good enough. From then on, life carried on for me in an uphill battle, where I perceived myself as being unworthy and inadequate. Yet, I forged ahead over the years, giving all that I had and more to life, and sometimes exhausting myself in the process. In those all-important formative years, I was so indoctrinated in fear that it took the greater part of my adult life to build myself up and to like and accept myself just the way I am. I felt that I had to constantly prove to myself and to others that I was good enough.

It has taken me most of my lifetime to develop my personality, to come to know myself, to evolve into the person that I was meant to be, and to know that I *am* good enough.

I've experienced success both at work and in energetic sports such as aerobics, jogging, and swimming. Sports helped me to release the pent-up feelings I had unconsciously built up over my lifetime.

I became an aerobics instructor, for which I had to sit exams, and I taught physical exercise and jogging techniques. I ran many mini-marathons, my ambition being to run for one hour without stopping, which I achieved many times. And I took life-saving lessons. Yet, I always had trouble rejoicing in my successes. Instead, I would adopt a matter-of-fact approach, telling myself that it was only because I had worked hard to achieve; nothing more, nothing less. The feelings of pleasure and happiness in having succeeded always eluded me. My attitude was always 'okay, now that's done, onto the next thing. One door has closed, now I will open another.'

I went through life feeling a deep-seated anger and hatred towards Miss Keane. How dare she treat me the way she did, and take her anger out on me, a small innocent child? And I continue to ask the question, what on earth was going on in this young woman's mind to persist in systematically beating me, trying to crush my spirit with such disdain, persisting in sheer evil acts, as she did, and abusing me? She is the only one who holds the answer to that, but I believe she did it simply because she could, and she had a propensity to cruelty.

I also experienced anger at the Dominican school. How could they have allowed this to happen? How could so many have participated in such evil? How could so many so-called good teachers keep silent, stand by, witness, and accept this cruelty? Why did the government agree to sanction corporal punishment at our schools? The Irish government and the Dominican Order of nuns failed us completely. Where was the national outcry of condemnation? It is my personal opinion that all of our teachers, whether or not they were perpetrators of abuse, failed us abused children totally, utterly, and without exception, by their very silence – a form of collusion.

A few years ago, I saw a video on a Ballyfermot Heritage website of a former nun talking about the good times she'd had there. I felt revolted. I wrote to her, providing an account of my own experience, and raising questions about how the Dominicans had tolerated physical violence against young children in the school. How did they allow excessive corporal punishment to become so normal? And why had they, as the nuns in charge, allowed it to continue for so long? She wrote back offering me therapy. I had expected an apology.

What therapy, I wonder, is there for the culture of silence? We Irish are resilient, expert at putting on a brave face and getting on with things, but this culture of silence is not good for our mental health or for the health of society. Silence is not the answer. It is my own personal experience of abuse that motivates me now to want to have my voice heard and to encourage those silent survivors to speak out, lest we take to our graves our own individual stories of abuse which are in themselves intertwined with the history and experience of education in Ballyfermot.

There can be no therapeutic closure or healing until the proper authorities acknowledge their role – their guilt as perpetrators; their guilt as silent observers. The lack of accountability means that feelings remain raw, people are still hurting, and an anger deep within still persists over 60 years later. People who were abused in school, physically and otherwise, deserve better. They deserve to go to the grave knowing that justice was done. Their families, parents, brothers, sisters, partners, and children, also deserve to have this justice, to know that behind the torment they witnessed in their loved ones was an explanation, an acknowledgement, and finally an apology.

Miss Keane gave each girl a holy picture to celebrate our confirmation, and she wrote a personal note on each one. Mine read: *To Brenda on your confirmation day, from Anne Keane, 30/3/1965.* I was 11 years old.

It was our habit to keep holy pictures in our confirmation prayer books, and I placed mine there. Although my prayer book didn't stand the test of time, I kept my holy picture for the best part of 40 years. But one night at my home in London, I decided to purge myself of this woman once and for all. I held a little ceremony all on my own. I took my holy picture and lit the corner of it with a match, then held it as it burned right down to my finger and thumb, and until the ash finally fell into the ashtray. It felt like the right thing to do at that moment in time.

I thought I might feel cleansed and be rid of her forever, but alas, one small act could not erase a lifetime of her negative presence, and her shadow persisted in following me. I guess you cannot just magic things away by one symbolic, purgative act! It does help, but a more collective act of cleansing is required.

My Poetry

My flight

Soaring high, leaving others behind,
A bird that won't be caged.
But for the loneliness
All is right.
Where is the other who soars as high?
Alas, nowhere in sight!
Tomorrow, another time, maybe then he'll try,
Two birds eclipsed in the skies, soaring high.
The one who soars beckons.
Infinite, insurmountable pleasure!
Soaring at her will!
Swooping over mountains and endless land
Nothing too great to measure!
Unlock the cage! Attempt the flight!
Join her in her triumph!
Feel the freedom of the skies!
BUT
If the flight be too great, then leave it,
let her soar alone.
Don't clip her wing to reach her,
THAT eclipse was never meant to be.

Written: 1984

An extension of me

One day I'll breathe into the world
An extension of me.
A child perhaps, a sonnet,
Something of high degree.
Some planned idea to remind the world
That once I took my place,
I'll leave behind a memory
An imprint not defaced.
I cannot go until the time
My extension is steadfast.
As yet this phase eludes me
And time is hurrying past.
But I will know the very hour,
Mere breath will tell me so.
My life is now completed,
My extension left to grow.
Then in contentment I'll come to You
And start again my life anew.
Of what importance? you ridicule,
Why has this to be?
The purpose of my life, my friend,
Is an extension of me.

Written: 1984

My mother taught me happiness

Wide awake! Up with the lark!
Her singing not far off.
Pull back the curtains! Make the beds!
Time for breakfast!
Sweeping brush at the ready,
All stations go!
Rise n' shine, daughter dear!
The sun is out, the day is here!
And
She sings!

Her happiness infectious
Neighbours too comment,
"Mrs Moore is singing!"
We smile, we feel content.
Her singing is quite beautiful
Ears twitch to hear her sound
She draws us in with every word
So lovely, so profound!

She takes us to another level
A place of happy din
Uplifted now, happy too,
Calm, we drink it in.

Mrs Moore is cheerful
In her garden now
Hanging out her washing,
She sings,
"If I had my life to live over
I would still do the same things again…"

Joy personified, captured, and enraptured,
I listen from my window
And then,
I sing!

Written: 2020

Ms Breda Joy

Copies fly across the room!
Fall on every desk!
Some sliding to the floor!
With heavy heart and in disgust
She shouts,
Teach you? If I really must!

Up and down the rows of desks
Angrily she trod!
Throwing papers down!
In silence, we froze.

And then she made her case:
I must teach two years in one!
Sixth year students with no base!

One with treasures to impart
She came upon our sleeping class.

Ms Breda Joy is a pseudonym

Time went on and we progressed
As time went on, I gleamed
Shakespeare's sonnets, prose and plays
We battled on a year of days.

She tore into every nuance
Bit by bit
Her depth of knowledge awe-inspiring
Reeling now with every word
My hunger grew!

A window opened in my mind
I'd not seen thru' before
With every day that passed
I wanted more!

As time went by, I spied
glimpses of what she taught
The joy she fostered never waned
The joy of learning remained.

Shakespeare's sonnets, prose and plays
Ever stayed throughout my days
And I would sing her praises
And I remember still
Ms Breda Joy.

                                              Written: 2020

---

*Ms Joy was the teacher who made the greatest impact on me. She was my English teacher for my last year at secondary school, which was at the age of 17 years. By that time, 1971, corporal punishment had long been abolished. I am appreciative to this day that I was lucky enough to have her enter my world.

The truth, the whole truth

One day the truth will out
This I know for sure.
An ugly past long buried
Will rise up to the fore.

Everything is hidden now
In Pandora's box, it's locked.
One day the truth will out
And release what's there, that's blocked.

One day the truth will out for some
We hold the very key
Pandora's box will open
If not by you then by me.

We'll give permission to the world
To view what has been hidden
The hurt, the pain, the anger
The life led – unforgiving!

For how could a child forgive
Teachers there to guide?
When all the while we lived
And corporal punishment abide!

To think of babes but six years old
And little more besides
Be beaten, slapped with hand and stick
By those who were our guide!

Sad, unhappy little one
I begged to God on high
Every day that passed
Why, God, why?

Always quite a good girl
Ever slow to offend
But she made me out as naughty
And the beatings never end.

Imprisoned in her classroom
Her lessons taught babe hate.
The pain severe on hands and legs
Treated just as meat.

Blackboard pointer, hand, and stick
She had them at the ready
At her mercy, I would cry,
"Please God, help me!" but
God was busy.

One day the truth will out
Our stories will reveal
With love and care
Should babes go forth
And not their happiness steal!

                                          Written: 2020

Margaret Oakes Maher
St Raphael's Primary School
Dominican Convent, Ballyfermot, Dublin
Abused 1962–1965
3rd, 4th & 5th class

Sadly, Brenda's story is in no way unique, just one of many abuse stories that has come to the fore over the decades. My own story of abuse was at the hands of one particular Dominican nun whose main pleasure in life was not to teach but to abuse small children, physically and mentally. This nun was small in stature but with the biggest mouth full of venom and loathing where, in her classroom, we children were reduced to quivering wrecks. Thinking back, I was one of the lucky ones in my class who didn't receive the worst of the physical abuse but I was often the object of the most deplorable and degrading mental abuse which has left scars that have remained with me to this day. Those three long years with the 'Nun from Hell' certainly contributed to many years where I struggled with severe anxiety and panic attacks. Many of my school friends with whom I am still friends today, have similar stories of torturous treatment at the hands of both lay and religious teachers at St Raphael's School, Dominican Convent, Ballyfermot, Dublin. It is totally devastating what we went through at the hands of these utter sadists whose main mission in life was to instill fear into the children they were meant to teach. We are so thankful to Brenda Moore for making her story known as it is also the story of many of us.

Education at the Dominican Convent Schools in Ballyfermot in the 50s/60s/70s
Rita Tighe, Dublin, Ireland

Ballyfermot in Dublin consisted mainly of large working class families. Its teachers were a mix of secular and religious, most of whom were from outside of Dublin. There was a divide between rural and city and between working class and middle class. There was an innate snobbery present in the teaching profession of that time. The girls who were better off than others were often favoured by the teacher. Back then corporal punishment was an intrinsic part of the teaching methodology. I recall going to school with a knot in my stomach every morning in the expectation that it was my turn for the stick that day. In my class, there was a secrecy imposed by the teacher around what went on in the classroom. If you did tell your parents about unfair beatings and such like, the standard response would have been that you probably deserved it. Control was handed over lock, stock and barrel to the teachers 'who knew best'. The parents who did protest about the severity of the abuse carried out on their children, were thought of as common, rough and unappreciative.

Of the 60 girls in my class at primary school, only 12 went on to second level which became free that year. I would suggest that the endurance test of primary school for so many played a role in these low numbers.

"In Irish Society, we have done a lot of looking back and clearly there is more to come, particularly about schools. This brief account of life and education in Ballyfermot, Dublin, during the 1960s is an important story. Not only does Brenda Moore paint a vivid picture of the 'daymare' of schoolteacher violence and bullying but in her story about overcoming adversity, she reminds us that people can and do move on."

Barry Cullen, Rialto, Dublin.

Milton Keynes UK
Ingram Content Group UK Ltd.
UKHW010202230823
427286UK00001B/1

9 781803 814513